FOR THE LOVE OF SPORTS
ARCHERY

Yolanda Ridge

www.openlightbox.com

Step 1
Go to www.openlightbox.com

Step 2
Enter this unique code

XUGQH3M2T

Step 3
Explore your interactive eBook!

CONTENTS
4 What Is Archery?
6 Getting Ready to Play
8 The Archery Range
9 World Archery Championships
10 Keeping Score
12 Rules of the Range
14 Playing the Game
16 History of Archery
18 Superstars of Archery
20 Staying Healthy
22 The Archery Quiz

AV2 is optimized for use on any device

Your interactive eBook comes with...

Contents
Browse a live contents page to easily navigate through resources

Audio
Listen to sections of the book read aloud

Videos
Watch informative video clips

Weblinks
Gain additional information for research

Slideshows
View images and captions

Try This!
Complete activities and hands-on experiments

Key Words
Study vocabulary, and complete a matching word activity

Quizzes
Test your knowledge

Share
Share titles within your Learning Management System (LMS) or Library Circulation System

Citation
Create bibliographical references following APA, CMOS, and MLA styles

This title is part of our AV2 digital subscription

1-Year Grades K–5 Subscription
ISBN 978-1-7911-3320-7

Access hundreds of AV2 titles with our digital subscription.
Sign up for a FREE trial at www.openlightbox.com/trial

FOR THE LOVE OF SPORTS
ARCHERY

CONTENTS

- 2 Interactive eBook Code
- 4 What Is Archery?
- 6 Getting Ready to Play
- 8 The Archery Range
- 9 World Archery Championships
- 10 Keeping Score
- 12 Rules of the Range
- 14 Playing the Game
- 16 History of Archery
- 18 Superstars of Archery
- 20 Staying Healthy
- 22 The Archery Quiz
- 23 Key Words/Index

What Is Archery?

Archery is the art of shooting arrows from a bow. Historically, archery was used for hunting and fighting. Ancient Egyptians, Greeks, and Chinese also practiced it as a sport.

Wars in Asia were won by archers on horseback. English soldiers used **longbows** that were sometimes as tall as they were. However, as time passed, the introduction of gunpowder made archery less common in battle. However, bows and arrows continued to be used as hunting weapons.

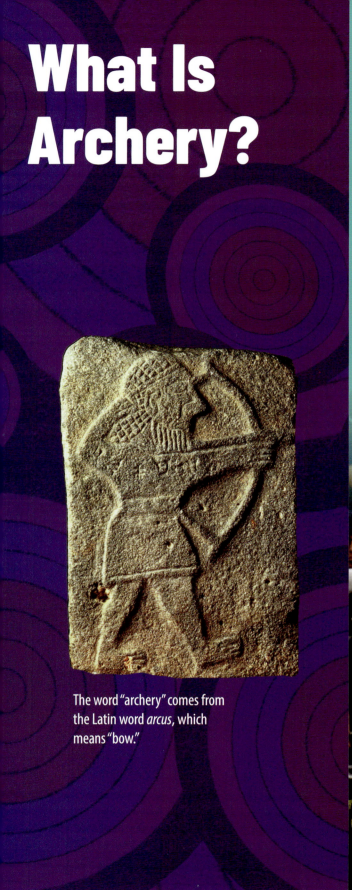

The word "archery" comes from the Latin word *arcus*, which means "bow."

4 For the Love of Sports

In the 1700s, archery became a fashionable sport in many countries. Archery societies were set up across England. Nobles and members of the royal family participated in events. By the 1800s, the modern sport of archery had spread to other parts of the world.

Archery was an Olympic event in 1900, 1904, 1908, and 1920. Then, after several decades without being included, it returned in 1972. This time, it became a permanent Olympic sport.

Archery is a sport that can be enjoyed by people of all ages and abilities.

A longbow can shoot an arrow more than 900 feet (275 meters).

At the 1988 Olympics, 14-year-old Denise Parker became the youngest person to win an Olympic medal in archery.

Archery was one of the first Olympic sports to include an event for women.

Archery 5

Getting Ready to Play

There are different types of bows used in archery. All of them have a string attached to a thin piece of material. The string holds the material in a curved position. Bows can be made of wood, plastic, or fiberglass.

Arrows can also be made of different materials. The long, thin part of an arrow is called the shaft. Traditionally, it was made of wood. The arrows used in modern archery are often made of aluminum or carbon fiber. One end of the arrow has a sharp tip. The other has plastic fins or a tail of feathers. The tail helps the arrow fly straight.

Arrow tails, sometimes called fletchings, come in a variety of shapes and sizes. Plastic fins replaced feathers for the first time in 1951.

Archers use quivers to hold arrows. Quivers can be worn with a belt around the waist or on the back with a shoulder strap. Ground quivers are designed to sit on the ground.

Bows vary in length according to the archer's height.

Gloves or tabs protect the fingers that an archer uses to pull a bow's string. The gloves are typically made of a smooth material, such as leather.

An arm guard is worn around an archer's elbow. It provides protection from the bowstring as the archer releases it.

Clothes worn by archers should be comfortable but not too loose-fitting. Long-sleeved shirts with buttons are not recommended.

Archery 7

The Archery Range

One of the most popular archery events is called target archery. In target archery, archers shoot at a round target that does not move. The distance between the archer and the target depends on skill level and bow type.

Archery ranges can be found indoors or outdoors. There is usually a **waiting line** and **shooting line**. Targets are set up at different distances. A side safety area is typically found on either side of the target range. Beyond the targets is an **overshoot line**. For safety purposes, people can only go into the side safety areas and overshoot zone when no one is shooting.

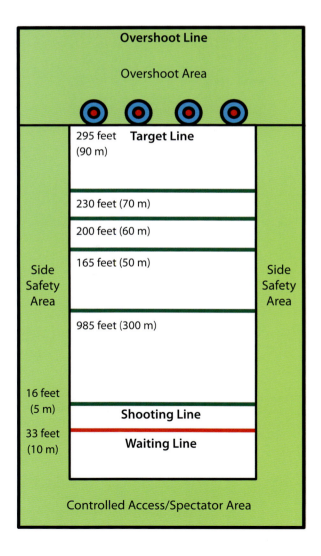

For the Love of Sports

World Archery Championships

There are many archery tournaments held around the world, featuring different types of events. **World Archery** held its first World Target Championships in 1931. Other major tournaments include the Mokrice World Archery 3D Championship and the World Archery Field Championships.

Germany
In 2023, the World Outdoor Target Championships took place in Berlin, Germany. There were 537 competitors from 81 countries. The results helped determine who competed in the 2024 Summer Olympics.

Keeping Score

The two most common types of bows used in target archery are **recurve** and **compound**. Recurve bows have tips at each end that curve away from the archer. Compound bows have pulleys, cables, and wheels. Both designs help the bow shoot arrows farther and faster.

Recurve archers tend to shoot at large targets from a distance. In compound archery, the target is closer and smaller. The target has 10 rings in both versions of the sport. Points are awarded based on which ring the arrow hits. Hitting the innermost circle, known as the bullseye, usually earns 10 points. The outermost ring earns one point. Missing the target earns zero points.

In the most common archery stance, feet are shoulder width apart and parallel to the shooting line. The front of the archer's body does not face the target.

Archery competitions are usually divided into rounds. During a round, archers shoot a certain number of arrows at the target. Points are added up once the round is finished. In compound archery, the score is determined by the total number of points. In recurve archery, an archer's score is based on whether he or she had more points than the opponent in each round. The winner is the archer who wins the most rounds.

Recurve archery uses a traditional style of bow.

Compound archery was invented in the United States in the 1960s. Pulleys and cables give a compound bow more power and precision.

Archery 11

Rules of the Range

To ensure safety, archers are expected to fire their bows carefully and properly. In the **ready position**, the side of an archer's body faces the target. Archers hold the bow in the hand closest to the target. Right-handed athletes usually hold the bow in their left hand. With the other hand, they place the tail end of the arrow on the bow string. This is called nocking the arrow.

There are several ways to draw a bow. For beginners, a three-finger draw works best. The joints of the fingers create a hook for the bowstring. The pointer finger goes above the arrow, while the middle and ring finger go below the arrow.

An arrow rest is often found above the part of a bow gripped by an archer. The arrow shaft sits there before the tail end is nocked. Some bows also have sight pins that help archers view the target.

12   **For the Love of Sports**

Once the arrow is nocked, the archer twists at the waist to direct the upper body and the arrow toward the target. The bow arm stays straight, while the other arm pulls the arrow and bow string back. This creates **tension** in the bow. The archer is ready to take aim.

When the arrow is in line with the target, the archer lets go of the bow string. The string jumps forward by itself when tension is released. The arrow flies toward the target. How far it goes depends on how far the archer draws the bow string.

Archers must have at least one foot behind the shooting line.

The bow string fits into a notch at the tail end of the arrow.

Archery 13

Playing the Game

As a sport, archery is open to everyone. It is one of the few sports where athletes with and without disabilities may compete against each other in the same events. Archers participate in many different versions of the sport. Target archery is part of the Olympic Games, Paralympic Games, World Archery Championships, and Archery World Cup. Competitions at the Olympic Games use the recurve bow. Compound archery is part of the World Archery Championships, Archery World Cup, and other events, including the Asian Games.

Archery requires precision, control, focus, repetition, and determination. Archers learn to "Focus-Aim-Release!"

Archery has been an event in every Paralympic Games since they started in 1960.

14 For the Love of Sports

International target archery competitions have individual, team, and mixed team events. A team is made up of three men or three women. A mixed team has one woman and one man. Team members all shoot with the same type of bow.

The World Archery Rankings were developed in 2001. Archers collect points for these rankings by competing in major tournaments held by World Archery. The rankings help determine whether an archer can compete in the World Cup Final.

There are three to four stages in the World Cup. In the final event, eight archers compete in each of four categories. These are women's recurve, men's recurve, women's compound, and men's compound. Winners are awarded the title of Hyundai Archery World Cup Champion.

Compound bows can shoot an arrow up to about 1,000 feet (305 m).

If an arrow splits another one that has already landed in the inner circle of a target, it is called a Robin Hood.

Archery 15

History of Archery

Archery is one of the oldest sports still practiced today. The first arrows were likely used for hunting. Over time, more advanced arrows, bows, and techniques were developed. Wars between countries were fought with these bows and arrows. Skills first developed by hunters and soldiers are now used in the sport of archery.

Arrowheads made of animal bone have been found dating back to about 60,000 years ago.

16 For the Love of Sports

1583 The first known modern archery competition is held in England.

1676 The Royal Company of Archers is formed in Scotland. It is one of the oldest sporting groups in the United Kingdom.

1900 Archery is included as a sport in the modern Olympics for the first time.

1931 The Fédération Internationale de Tir à l'Arc, or Federation of International Target Archery, is formed in what is now Lviv, Ukraine. The organization standardizes international rules and later becomes known as World Archery.

1972 After more than 50 years, archery is reintroduced to the Olympics. It has been an Olympic event ever since.

2024 A total of 128 archers, from 53 different countries, compete in archery events at the Olympic Games in Paris.

More than 160 countries have national archery federations.

Hubert Van Innis competed in the 1900 and 1920 Olympic Games. He won a record-setting nine Olympic medals in archery.

There are about 30 million archers around the world.

Archery 17

Superstars of Archery

Archery greats from all over the world inspire players to take up the sport.

Darrell Pace
BIRTH DATE: October 23, 1956
HOMETOWN: Cincinnati, Ohio

CAREER FACTS:
- Darrell won his first U.S. National Championship in 1973. He then went on to win the next three in a row.
- In 1975, Darrell won his first World Archery Championship.
- Darrell went to the Olympics for the first time in 1976 when he was 19 years old. He won a gold medal in the individual event.
- In 2011, Darrell was named Male Archer of the 20th Century by World Archery.

Lida Scott Howell
BIRTH DATE: August 28, 1859
HOMETOWN: Lebanon, Ohio

CAREER FACTS:
- Lida won the Ohio State Archery Championships in 1881 and 1882.
- Between 1883 and 1907, Lida competed in 20 U.S. National Championships. She won 17 of these competitions.
- Lida held the record for best score in a U.S. National Championship for 36 years.
- Lida won three gold medals in the 1904 Olympics. At the time, archery was the only sport women were allowed to enter.
- In 1975, Lida was inducted into the Archery Hall of Fame.

Kim Soo-Nyung
BIRTH DATE: April 5, 1971
HOMETOWN: Chungbeongbuk, South Korea

CAREER FACTS:
- Kim made the Korean National Team when she was only about 16 years old.
- In 1988, Kim won two Olympic gold medals. She went on to win four more Olympic medals in 1992 and 2000.
- Kim won gold medals in both individual and team events at the World Archery Championship in 1989 and 1991.
- In 2011, Kim was named Female Archer of the 20th Century by World Archery.

For the Love of Sports

Matt Stutzman

BIRTH DATE: December 10, 1982
HOMETOWN: Kansas City, Kansas

CAREER FACTS:
- Matt was a silver medalist at the London Paralympic Games in 2012.
- In 2015, Matt hit a target 930 feet (283 m) away. It broke a record for longest distance shot by any archer in the world.
- Matt won the individual compound competition at the 2022 Para World Championships in Dubai.
- In 2022, Matt was named Para Archer of the Year by World Archery.
- Matt won a gold medal at the Paris Paralympic Games in 2024. It was his fourth time competing in the Paralympic Games.

Im Dong-Hyun

BIRTH DATE: May 12, 1986
HOMETOWN: Chungbuk, South Korea

CAREER FACTS:
- Im was a member of the Korean national team for 18 years.
- When he was 18 years old, Im became archery's youngest male champion by winning gold in the team competition at the 2004 Athens Olympic Games.
- Im won his first World Championships in 2007.
- Legally blind, Im retired from competition in 2021. He returned to the 2024 Olympic Games as a coach for the Korean team.

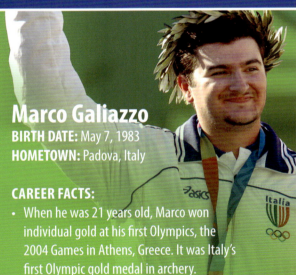

Marco Galiazzo

BIRTH DATE: May 7, 1983
HOMETOWN: Padova, Italy

CAREER FACTS:
- When he was 21 years old, Marco won individual gold at his first Olympics, the 2004 Games in Athens, Greece. It was Italy's first Olympic gold medal in archery.
- Over his career, Marco went to the Olympics four times, winning two gold medals and one silver medal.
- In 2023, Marco was honored with a plaque on Italy's sporting Walk of Fame in Rome.

Lim Si-Hyeon

BIRTH DATE: June 13, 2003
HOMETOWN: Gangneung, South Korea

CAREER FACTS:
- At the 2022 Asian Games, Lim won three gold medals.
- Lim joined the Korean national team in 2023.
- Lim was named Female Archer of the Year for 2023 by World Archery.
- In her Olympic debut at the 2024 Games in Paris, Lim won gold medals in all three of her events.
- Lim was ranked the number one female recurve archer in 2024.

Archery 19

Staying Healthy

Archery is very safe. The chance of getting injured is lower than most other sports. Wearing protective equipment helps prevent injuries. Using bows and arrows that are the right size reduces the risk of muscle strain and joint pain. Warm-ups, stretching, and strengthening exercises are also helpful. They should target the shoulders, back, arms, and core.

Arrows should not be removed from a target or the ground until all archers on the range have finished shooting.

High-protein food, such as meat, peanut butter, or eggs, can help repair muscles and give archers the energy needed to compete.

It is a good idea for beginners to take an introductory archery course. It is also important to know the rules of the range. Rules can be different depending on the course setup. Most use a whistle system to let archers know when to shoot and when to stop shooting.

Most people participate in archery for enjoyment and as a social activity. However, the **professional** athletes that compete at the highest level dedicate hours to training every day , shooting thousands of arrows a year. As with other sports, staying active and eating a well-balanced diet improves performance and overall health.

The most common archery injuries are caused by repetition. Proper stretching and muscle training can help prevent these injuries.

THE ARCHERY QUIZ

- 1 - When did archery **first** become an Olympic event?

- 2 - What do archers use to hold their **arrows**?

- 3 - What does the **Latin word** *arcus* mean?

- 4 - What is one of the **most popular** archery events?

- 5 - Which type of bow uses **pulleys** and **cables**?

- 6 - Where were the **World Outdoor Target Championships** held in 2023?

- 7 - How many **rings** do recurve and compound archery targets have?

- 8 - What type of bow is used at archery **events** in the **Olympics**?

- 9 - When were the **World Archery Rankings** developed?

- 10 - Who was the **Female Archer of the Year** in 2023?

ANSWERS: **1** 1900 **2** Quivers **3** "Bow" **4** Target archery **5** Compound **6** Berlin, Germany **7** 10 **8** Recurve **9** 2001 **10** Lim Si-Hyeon

22 For the Love of Sports

Key Words

compound: in archery, a type of bow that uses cables and pulleys

longbows: tall bows, traditionally made from single pieces of wood

overshoot line: an area beyond the target range where arrows might go if they miss the targets

professional: taking part in an activity or sport as a job

ready position: the stance taken by archers when they are ready to shoot

recurve: in archery, a traditional style of bow with tips that curve away from the archer

shooting line: a line drawn on the field or ground that shows where archers stand when shooting

tension: the state of being stretched tight

waiting line: a line drawn on the field or ground that shows where archers go when they are done shooting or when they are waiting to shoot

World Archery: the federation that organizes international tournaments and calculates player rankings

Index

Archery World Cup 14, 15
Asian Games 14, 19

compound archery 10, 11, 14, 15, 19, 22

Galiazzo, Marco 19

Howell, Lida Scott 18

Im Dong-Hyun 19

Kim Soo-Nyung 18

Lim Si-Hyeon 19, 22
longbow 4, 5

Olympics 5, 9, 14, 17, 18, 19, 22

Pace, Darrell 18
Paralympic Games 14, 19
Parker, Denise 5

recurve archery 10, 11, 14, 15, 19, 22

Stutzman, Matt 19

target archery 8, 10, 14, 15, 17, 22

Van Innis, Hubert 17

World Archery 9, 15, 17, 18, 19, 22
World Archery Championships 9, 14, 18

Archery 23

Get the best of both worlds.
AV2 bridges the gap between print and digital.

The expandable resources toolbar enables quick access to content including videos, audio, activities, **weblinks**, **slideshows**, **quizzes**, and **key words**.

Animated videos make static images come alive.

Resource icons on each page help readers to further **explore key concepts**.

Published by Lightbox Learning Inc.
276 5th Avenue, Suite 704 #917
New York, NY 10001
Website: www.openlightbox.com

Copyright ©2026 Lightbox Learning Inc.
All rights reserved. No part of this publication may be reproduced, stored in a retrieval system, or transmitted in any form or by any means, electronic, mechanical, photocopying, recording, or otherwise, without the prior written permission of the publisher.

Library of Congress Control Number: 2025931412

ISBN 979-8-8745-2644-3 (hardcover)
ISBN 979-8-8745-2645-0 (softcover)
ISBN 979-8-8745-2646-7 (static multi-user eBook)
ISBN 979-8-8745-2647-4 (interactive multi-user eBook)

Printed in Guangzhou, China
1 2 3 4 5 6 7 8 9 0   29 28 27 26 25

012025
101124

Project Coordinator John Willis
Art Director Terry Paulhus
Layout Jean Faye Rodriguez

Photo Credits
Every reasonable effort has been made to trace ownership and to obtain permission to reprint copyright material. The publisher would be pleased to have any errors or omissions brought to its attention so that they may be corrected in subsequent printings. The publisher acknowledges Alamy, Getty Images, Shutterstock, and Wikimedia as its primary image suppliers for this title.

View new titles and product videos at www.openlightbox.com